WELL

TRAVEL GUIDE 2024

The Comprehensive Guide to Exploring
Landmarks, Heritage, and Hidden Gems, Alongside
Insider Tips for an Unforgettable Adventure

CURZIO MANNA

TABLE OF CONTENTS

INTRODUCTION

Wellington, the vibrant capital of New
Zealand, offers a unique blend of urban
sophistication and scenic beauty, situated
between undulating hills and a stunning
harbor. Often referred to as the "Coolest
Little Capital in the World," this dynamic
city captivates travelers seeking a wide
range of experiences. Wellington delivers an

amazing experience, from its rich cultural scene to outdoor excursions and gastronomic pleasures.

Wellington Overview

Wellington, New Zealand's political, cultural, and artistic hub, is situated on the southwest corner of the country's North Island. The city, which has about 500,000 residents, is characterized by a compact urban design that is encircled by hills and a ruggcd coastline. Wellington's breathtaking scenery is enhanced by its picturesque location, which faces the Pacific Ocean to the east and south and the Tasman Sea to the west.

The blend of modern and historic buildings in the cityscape illustrates Wellington's development from a colonial outpost to a major international city. The famous Wellington Cable Car traverses the landscape on its ascent from Lambton Quay to Kelburn, offering expansive views.

One of Wellington's most distinctive features is the harbor, a bustling waterfront area that offers a range of activities, from strolls to water sports. Te Papa Tongarewa, the country's museum, is positioned majestically along the waterfront and symbolizes the city's commitment to preserving and promoting New Zealand's natural and cultural heritage.

Wellington's weather is renowned for being cyclical, with four distinct seasons. Six to twelve degrees Celsius (43 to 54 degrees Fahrenheit) are the typical winter temperatures, while summer temperatures range from 20 to 25 degrees Celsius (68 to 77 degrees Fahrenheit). Because of its ever-changing weather, the city is known for having "four seasons in one day," which adds to the surprise factor of visiting visitors' experiences.

Why Go to Wellington?

The multifaceted charm of Wellington appeals to a wide range of interests, which is the source of its fascination. Some compelling arguments for Wellington as your next holiday spot are as follows:

With an exceptional array of museums, galleries, and theaters, Wellington is the cultural hub of New Zealand. Maori culture, art, and history are all on display at Te Papa Tongarewa, New Zealand's national museum. World-class performances are presented in Wellington's theaters, like the St. James Theatre and the Circa Theatre, providing a haven for those who enjoy the arts and culture.

Surrounded by hills and a craggy shoreline, Wellington boasts spectacular natural splendor. There are expansive views over the city, port, and surrounding area from the summit of Mount Victoria. The Wellington Botanic Garden, perched on the hillsides of the city, offers a peaceful retreat with its abundant flora and floral displays.

Outdoor Activities: There are plenty of outdoor activities available in Wellington for adventurers. The city offers hiking trails like the Southern Walkway and beachside bicycle lanes to suit the needs of people who want an active lifestyle. The nearby Rimutaka Forest Park and Matiu/Somes Island offer more opportunities for nature exploration.

Culinary Delights: Wellington's diverse culinary culture appeals to a wide range of palates, earning it the reputation of a culinary haven. Even the pickiest palates will be pleased by the city's culinary options, which include everything from upscale dining establishments to unique cafés and bustling food markets.

Film and Creativity: Wellington has ties to the film industry because of Weta Workshop, a globally recognized special effects and prop company. Cinema enthusiasts may experience the behind-the-scenes magic of popular films like "The Lord of the Rings" and "Avatar" by visiting the Weta Cave and participating in guided tours.

Given its compact size, Wellington is a great city to explore on foot because it's quite walkable. Urban exploration opportunities abound in bustling places like Courtenay Place and Cuba Street, which have unique businesses, street art, and a vibrant atmosphere.

Best time to visit

The ideal time to visit Wellington depends on your preferences and the kind of experience you are looking for. Nonetheless, a few general suggestions could help travelers organize their trip well.

a. Summer (December to February): This time of year is ideal for outdoor activities because of the pleasant temperatures and long daylight hours. The city comes alive in the summer with festivals, events, and energy. It is perfect for outdoor activities like hiking and beach visits.

b. Autumn (March to May): Autumn is a beautiful time of year to explore because of the gorgeous foliage and lower temps. It's the ideal time to explore the city's culinary options, go on nature excursions, and attend cultural events.

c. Winter (June to August): Wellington's climate is still pleasant compared to other places, even though the winters are colder. Winter is a great time of year for indoor pursuits like going to plays and museums and sampling the local cuisine.

d. Spring (September to November): The blossoming of flowers and the revitalization of the surroundings greet the city as it awakens from its winter hibernation. It's a great time to go horseback riding, take in the cultural offerings of the city, and explore the botanical gardens.

Lastly, Wellington's year-round attraction ensures that, come rain or shine, there's always something fresh to discover. Visitors should think about their interests and the specific activities they wish to partake in while deciding whether or not to visit this fascinating city.

GETTING TO WELLINGTON

Wellington is easily accessible by air and sea, whether you're traveling around New Zealand or are arriving from another nation. Arriving in Wellington is a hassle-free journey that sets the stage for an amazing experience in the vibrant capital, thanks to a well-connected airport and ferry links linking the city to the South Island.

By Air

Wellington International Airport

The main entry to the capital city is Wellington International Airport, which is located about 8 kilometers (5 miles) southeast of the downtown business center. The Cook Strait and gorgeous hills surround the airport, which accepts both domestic and international travelers.

a. Domestic Flights

Domestic flights offer a quick and effective way to get from Wellington to major cities in New Zealand. Wellington to Auckland, Christchurch, Queenstown, and other regional cities are regularly served by flights operated by Air New Zealand, Jetstar, and Sounds Air. Because of the short journey times, domestic air travel is an alluring option for those who want to see the various landscapes of the North and South Islands.

b. International Flights:

Wellington International Airport handles international flights, particularly those to and from Australia, despite its smaller size compared to some of New Zealand's other international airports. Wellington is easily accessible to foreign visitors thanks to its direct flights to cities like Sydney and Melbourne. Passing via Auckland or Christchurch is another common option for those coming from other countries.

c. Airport Services:

To ensure a comfortable and enjoyable journey, Wellington International Airport provides a range of amenities. The airport offers a wide range of services to meet the various needs of travelers, including restaurants and duty-free shopping, currency exchange, and car rental counters. The modern terminal and effective services further enhance Wellington's stellar reputation as a resort that welcomes tourists.

d. Transportation from the Airport:

There are numerous transportation options available to passengers landing at Wellington International Airport. There are plenty of taxis, shuttles, and rental cars available, so getting to the city center and other locations is simple. Public buses also connect the airport to other parts of Wellington, offering a quick and affordable means of transportation.

e. Tips for Air Travel to Wellington:

- Book Early: It is best to book flights as soon as possible to get the best deals and availability, especially during peak travel seasons.

- Flexible Arrival Times: Considering Wellington's erratic weather, it is a good idea to allow some leeway in your arrival plans to account for unforeseen weather-related issues.

By Sea

Ferry Services

For a really beautiful and laid-back experience, taking a boat to Wellington is an alluring substitute. A unique perspective of New Zealand's breathtaking shoreline beauty is offered by the Interislander and Bluebridge ferry services, which connect Wellington with the South Island. The Cook Strait passage is an adventure unto itself, not just a means of transportation.

a. Interislander Ferry:
Travel between the North and South Islands is frequently accomplished using Interislander ferries. Travelers can enjoy breathtaking views of the Marlborough Sounds as the boat glides over Cook Strait, departing from Wellington. It ends in the picturesque settlement of Picton, which is located close to the top of the South Island.

b. Bluebridge Ferry:
Using a similar route between Wellington and Picton, Bluebridge is another

well-known ferry service. Like the Interislander, Bluebridge allows passengers to unwind and take in the surroundings while providing a comfortable and attractive ride over the Cook Strait. Passengers have options because both ferry services offer numerous sailings throughout the day.

c. Onboard facilities:

Taking a boat from Wellington to the South Island is an adventure on the water; it's not just a way to get around. There are plenty of food and drink options, cozy chairs, and panoramic viewing decks on board. Alternatively, passengers can choose to unwind on the exterior decks or indoors while admiring the breathtaking scenery.

d. Duration and Schedule:

Depending on the ferry service and the state of the sea, the boat trip from Wellington to Picton takes three to five hours. The itineraries are designed to accommodate a range of travel preferences, with multiple sailings offered throughout the day. Booking reservations in advance and checking boat schedules are advised, especially during peak travel times.

e. Transit and accessibility:

From Wellington's city center, it is quite easy to reach both the Interislander and Bluebridge ferry terminals. Efficient transit between the ferry terminals and other parts of the city is made possible by a variety of services, including taxis and shuttles. Those who want to explore Wellington's surroundings after disembarking can also take advantage of rental car options.

f. Tips for Ferry Travel to Wellington:
- Book Early: To ensure availability, it is advised to purchase ferry tickets well in advance, particularly during peak travel seasons.
- Enjoy the Views: Make the most of the boat ride to get a beautiful view of the Marlborough Sounds and Cook Strait. Outdoor viewing decks provide fantastic picture possibilities.
- Flexible plan: While ferry timings are typically dependable, it's best to have some wiggle room in your plan to account for unexpected weather-related effects on maritime travel.

Ultimately, reaching Wellington by plane or sea creates the conditions for an engaging and varied visit to the capital of New Zealand. Accessible Wellington International Airport and scenic boat cruises provide travelers with alternatives tailored to their interests, making the journey itself an essential component of the Wellington experience.

ACCOMMODATION OPTIONS IN WELLINGTON

Hotels

The hotel business in Wellington is friendly and diverse, serving a wide range of travelers from high rollers seeking rooms with views of the harbor to low-key travelers seeking cozy stays in the city center. There are many different hotel options in the capital city, and each one adds to a unique and memorable experience.

a. Luxury Hotels:

For travelers seeking a comfortable and elegant stay, Wellington's best hotels provide an opulent haven. With stunning views of the bay, the InterContinental Wellington on the waterfront offers spectacular rooms and suites. In addition, the QT Wellington offers a boutique experience right in the middle of the city by fusing luxury with modern artwork. Guests may expect personalized service, first-rate amenities, and excellent culinary options at these locations.

b. Mid-Range Hotels:

Wellington is renowned for having mid-range hotels that strike a balance between affordability and comfort. Situated on the busy Lambton Quay, the James Cook Hotel Grand Chancellor offers spacious accommodations with convenient access to the city's attractions. Another option for travelers is the Novotel Wellington, a contemporary hotel in a prime location that provides a relaxing holiday without going over budget.

c. Low-Cost Accommodations:

For those on a tight budget, Wellington offers a variety of affordable hotel options. Located in the heart of the city, Nomads Capital Backpackers provides lively social surroundings along with reasonably priced dorm-style lodging. With both private and shared room layouts, YHA Wellington City, part of the Youth Hostels Association, offers a neat and reasonably priced option.

d. Tips for Choosing Hotels in Wellington:

- Location is Important: Think about the Wellington location you have selected. Choose a hotel that corresponds to your exploring goals, whether it's on the seaside, in the city center, or in a certain area.

- Facilities: Ascertain the facilities that are most essential to you. Whether it is free Wi-Fi, on-site dining options, or a fitness center, make sure the hotel you have chosen meets your requirements for comfort and convenience.

- To find out more about the hotel's general cleanliness, level of service, and overall visitor experience, read reviews left by previous visitors.

Bed and Breakfast

Wellington offers a great selection of excellent bed & breakfast options for those seeking a more personal and tailored hotel experience. These locations, which are frequently run by residents, provide a friendly and inviting atmosphere that gives visitors the impression that they are a part of the neighborhood.

a. Local Hospitality:
Bed and breakfasts in Wellington are highly regarded for their warm reception. To provide insider knowledge about the area, point out hidden gems, and put guests at ease, hosts frequently go above and beyond. A bed and breakfast's sense of community and intimate connection set it apart from other forms of lodging.

b. Unique settings:
A lot of bed and breakfasts in Wellington are housed in old buildings or charming homes

which adds a unique element to the overall experience. Every property, whether they are modern townhouses or mansions from the Victorian era, offers a different setting that enhances the allure of the visit.

c. Homemade Breakfast:

As the name suggests, breakfast is the best part of staying at a bed and breakfast. Visitors can savor freshly produced meals prepared by their hosts with regional spices and produce. This unique touch makes staying at a bed and breakfast even more appealing.

d. Tips for Choosing Wellington Bed and Breakfasts:

- Engaging your hosts: Consider the level of interaction you desire. Some visitors prefer a more hands-on approach, while others desire more freedom.

- Location: To create a more tranquil atmosphere, bed and breakfasts are frequently found in residential areas. Confirm the closeness of the venue to your planned activities and attractions.

- Though they are frequently lovely and cozy, bed and breakfasts should be understood for the amenities they provide, like Wi-Fi, parking, and private restrooms.

Hostels

For those on a tight budget, traveling alone, or seeking a social setting, Wellington's hostels provide inexpensive shared accommodation. There are many different kinds and locations of hostels, but they all provide a vibrant, social environment for visitors to meet and exchange stories.

a. Dormitory-style Lodgings:

Hostels are a cost-effective travel choice because they frequently offer dormitory-style rooms with shared bathrooms. YHA Wellington City, Base Wellington, and The Dwellington are well-liked substitutes that offer a range of bed configurations in hygienic, comfortable dorms.

b. Social Climate:

One of the things that sets hostels apart is the social atmosphere. There are common areas, communal kitchens, and planned activities that let guests interact with other travelers. Because of its sociable attitude, hostels are an excellent choice for lone travelers or those seeking a more immersive experience.

c. Private Rooms Available:

Although hostels typically offer dorms, many also have separate rooms available for those who prefer a little more seclusion. This is the best choice for couples, friends traveling in groups, or anyone looking for a more sedate setting.

d. Tips for Choosing Hostels in Wellington:

- Environment: Consider the atmosphere you want. Some hostels are renowned for their party atmospheres, while others prefer a more relaxing and tranquil atmosphere.

- Check for important amenities like Wi-Fi, kitchen access, and laundry services. These extras may dramatically improve your stay.
- Location: There are hostels all across Wellington, so choose one that is in your favorite area or close to significant attractions.

Finally, Wellington's hotel options cater to a broad range of interests and budgets. Whether you like the sophistication of a hotel, the personal touch of a bed and breakfast, or the sociable atmosphere of a hostel, the city ensures that every guest has a pleasant and pleasurable stay.

TRANSPORTATION IN WELLINGTON

Public Transportation

Wellington's fast and well-connected public transport network makes exploring the city and its environs simple. Wellington offers convenient access to public transit for both locals and visitors, with options including buses, trains, and even a historic cable car.

a. Buses:

Wellington's public transit system is anchored by a vast bus network. The buses, which travel around the city and its suburbs and offer a reasonably priced and environmentally friendly way to move about Wellington, are operated by Metlink. Important locations like the central business district, the suburbs, and well-known tourist attractions are connected via the roadways. The buses, with their vibrant colors, are a common sight on Wellington's streets, providing a dependable and convenient means of transit.

b. Trains:

One excellent way to get around Wellington and its surroundings is by taking a trip on the suburban rail system. The bay and the surrounding landscape are magnificently viewed from the charming train tracks. The main hub is Wellington Railway Station, which connects several lines that extend to locations like Porirua, Lower Hutt, and Upper Hutt. Trains are a comfortable and effective form of transportation that runs all day.

c. Cable car:

The historic Wellington Cable Car is a unique and recognizable feature of Wellington's public transit system. In addition to being a quick and easy method to get to the Botanic Garden, the cable car that runs between Lambton Quay in the city center and Kelburn, offering breathtaking views of the harbor and city. The short journey, which combines practicality with a nostalgic touch, is a must-do for visitors.

d. Payment and Fares:

Passengers can easily transition between modes of transportation thanks to Metlink's standard pricing structure for buses, trains, and cable cars. The Snapper card is a contactless smart card that travelers can use to pay for their travel expenses. You can top off the card at any retail location in the city or online.

e. Accessibility:

People of all abilities can use Wellington's public transportation system. Elevators and ramps are seen in rail stations, whereas low floors on buses make boarding easier. Because of its commitment to accessibility, public transit is easily accessible to all residents of the city.

Ridesharing Services and Taxis

Although there is a lot of public transportation available, those who would rather travel in comfort can have a more personalized, door-to-door experience with taxis and ridesharing services.

a. Taxis:

In Wellington, traditional taxi services are easily available, and taxi stands are situated in busy areas, including the central business district and important transit hubs. For those who value convenience, taxis are an excellent quick and direct mode of transportation. Wellington's taxi service is renowned for its dependability and adherence to safety rules.

b. Ride-Sharing Services:

Ridesharing services, including Uber and Lyft, have become more and more common in Wellington, giving tourists an additional level of convenience. Customers may easily arrange trips, track the movements of their driver, and make cashless payments with these app-based services. Because rideshare services are frequently inexpensive, they present a compelling substitute for traditional taxis.

c. Safety and Accessibility:

Passenger safety and accessibility are given priority in Wellington taxis and ridesharing services. Background checks are performed on drivers, and cars are inspected frequently to ensure that safety standards are being met. Ridesharing is a more inclusive form of transportation because many of the vehicles are equipped to accommodate passengers with mobility impairments.

d. Airport Transportation:

For smooth transit to and from Wellington International Airport, taxis and ridesharing services are also commonly available. Passengers arriving may swiftly identify designated taxi ranks and rideshare pickup locations, which will speed up their journey to their hotel or other destinations.

Renting a Car

Renting a car offers people the flexibility and freedom to create a custom itinerary for their leisurely exploration of Wellington and its environs.

a. Rental Options:

A variety of car rental companies in Wellington offer a wide range of vehicles to accommodate different preferences and party sizes. From compact cars for single tourists to SUVs for groups of people, there are many rental options available. Well-known rental car companies Avis, Hertz, and Budget have convenient locations across the city and at the airport.

b. Beyond the City Exploration:

You can view the breathtaking landscape and other activities that are located outside of Wellington by renting a car. Traveling by car allows you to experience the various environments surrounding the city, ranging from the rugged Kapiti Coast coastline to the Wairarapa region's wineries.

c. Parking and Navigation:

Parking is available in Wellington on and off the street, while availability varies with time of day and location. Renting a car makes it simple to explore the suburbs and surrounding areas of the city and provides faster access to sites that could be challenging to get to by public transportation.

d. Considerations:

Before renting a car in New Zealand, it's important to comprehend the laws and rules governing the roads. Driving in this country is done on the left side of the road, and its diverse terrain may include winding roads and erratic weather. Renters must ensure that their driver's license is up to date and that they are aware of all applicable traffic laws.

In conclusion, Wellington's transportation options cater to a variety of preferences, allowing visitors to select the one that best suits their needs. Arriving in Wellington is a seamless and enjoyable experience, regardless of your preference for the convenience of public transportation, the individualized attention of taxis and ridesharing, or the independence of a rented car.

ATTRACTIONS AND SIGHTSEEING

Te Papa Tongarewa (National Museum)

Te Papa Tongarewa, the National Museum of New Zealand, is a cultural gem located along Wellington's waterfront that invites tourists to explore the history, artwork, and natural wonders of the nation. Te Papa Tongarewa, the museum's Maori name, means "container of treasures," an excellent description of an establishment that embodies the essence of New Zealand's distinctive history.

The nation's commitment to preserving and advancing its cultural diversity is embodied in Te Papa. Exhibitions that are one-of-a-kind and engage visitors on multiple levels accentuate the museum's modern style. A comprehensive perspective of New Zealand's past and present is offered by the galleries, which deftly combine topics of European colonization, Maori and Pacific

Islander cultures, and the natural environment.

The interactive displays at the museum, which let visitors of all ages and backgrounds interact with the exhibits, demonstrate the institution's commitment to diversity. With its immersive digital experiences and practical activities, Te Papa provides a lively and educational environment. The famous Colossal Squid, which is on display in the natural history section of the museum, is a prime example of the organization's dedication to showcasing extraordinary and uncommon artifacts.

Maori cultural performances and rituals take place at Te Marae at Te Papa, a vibrant and sacred space. To guarantee that Maori communities' cultural inheritance is appropriately reflected, the museum constantly collaborates with them, promoting dialogue and cooperation.

In addition to its permanent collection, Te Papa hosts rotating exhibitions that delve into contemporary issues, art movements, and scientific advancements. The museum's commitment to being dynamic and current enhances its reputation as a living institution that captures the changing face of New Zealand.

Wellington Cable Car

A spectacular and picturesque experience, the Wellington Cable Car is a local monument that offers more than just transportation. With breathtaking views of the city, harbor, and surrounding area, the cable car departs from Lambton Quay and travels across Wellington's verdant hills.

Wellington residents have been used to the red-coach Cable Car since its establishment in 1902. Even now, locals and tourists alike still flock to the Kelburn area because of this well-liked attraction. The five-minute ride allows passengers to take in the constantly shifting panorama through large windows.

Discover the Wellington Botanic Garden, another jewel in the city's crown, as soon as visitors arrive at Kelburn. The history and workings of this cherished mode of transportation are explained in the Cable Car Museum, which is located at the top. Using historical photos, interactive exhibits, and old cable cars, visitors are taken back in time to the early days of this technological marvel.

It's not only about the ride with the Cable Car. Wellington is popular with locals and photographers seeking the perfect cityscape because of its highest viewing locations, such as the Carter Observatory's overlook, which offers breathtaking views of the surrounding landscape.

Whether you use it to go to the garden or just for the ride itself, the Wellington Cable Car is a beloved part of the city's identity. Wellington's hilly landscape, commitment to preserving its history, and ideal fusion of tourism and pragmatism are all brought to mind by it.

Wellington Botanic Garden

Nestled on the hillsides above the city, the Wellington Botanic Garden offers a peaceful haven of unspoiled beauty. This enormous 25-hectare green park invites people to explore themed gardens, meander along charming walks, and take in the diverse flora while offering a break from the hustle and bustle of the city.

Visitors are enthralled by the vibrant and fragrant display of over 3,000 roses in the Lady Norwood Rose Garden. The exotic begonia and tropical plant collection is housed in the Victorian-style glasshouse known as Begonia House. The natural forest section displays the flora and fauna of New Zealand, including native trees, ferns, and mammals.

One landmark of the Wellington Botanic Garden is the eco-friendly Treehouse Visitor Centre, which provides information on the garden's history, conservation efforts, and upcoming events. Numerous walking paths begin at the Treehouse and wind across the many landscapes of the garden.

Experience something unique by taking the Wellington Cable Car, which connects Lambton Quay to the summit of Kelburn's garden. In addition to providing a convenient means of access to the garden, the cable car trip offers passengers breathtaking views of Wellington and its port.

In addition to being a beautiful natural setting, the Wellington Botanic Garden serves as a hub for culture and community. The garden is made more lively with outdoor concerts, art exhibits, and family-friendly activities, making it a desirable destination for both locals and visitors.

Lastly, the Wellington Botanic Garden is a prime example of the city's commitment to preserving natural areas and providing a sanctuary for lovers of the outdoors. Whether visitors come to the garden for a peaceful moment of relaxation, to explore themed gardens, or to begin stunning excursions, they are rewarded with a sensory journey through the various landscapes of New Zealand.

Weta Workshop

For movie buffs and anybody curious about the artistry of special effects, Weta Workshop is a must-visit location, situated in the artistic hub of Miramar. Founded by Sir Richard Taylor, Tania Rodger, and Peter Jackson, Weta Workshop has been instrumental in bringing to life some of the most well-known movies ever made, such as "Avatar," "King Kong," and "The Lord of the Rings" trilogy.

Weta Workshop offers guided tours that provide a fascinating behind-the-scenes look at the intricate processes involved in creating the costumes, props, and special effects for popular motion pictures. Sculpting, molding, and computer design are among the techniques used by seasoned artists to bring magical worlds to life for visitors to witness.

The company's store and gallery, The Weta Cave, serves as a portal into the cinematic worlds created by the Weta artists. Thanks to the exhibition of movie memorabilia, collectibles, and limited-edition reproductions, moviegoers can bring a piece of their favorite films home. Additionally, The Cave features interactive displays that let guests interact with the equipment and techniques utilized during filming.

Weta Workshop has an impact on the film industry as well as Wellington's vibrant creative community. The company regularly engages with the community through partnerships with up-and-coming artists, seminars, and educational programs.

For fans of film, a trip to Weta Workshop is an exploration of the creative and handcrafted realms. It's an opportunity to witness the magic that takes place behind the scenes, discover the cooperative nature of filmmaking, and be inspired by the passion of the incredible individuals who bring stories to life.

Zealandia Ecosanctuary

Wellington's Zealandia Ecosanctuary, which lies just outside the city limits, is a prime example of New Zealand's commitment to ecological restoration and conservation. This 225-hectare urban sanctuary provides a haven for native species while providing refuge for the natural flora and fauna.

The sanctuary's history is linked to the transformation of a reservoir into a fully enclosed, predator-free zone. Natural habitats of native birds, reptiles, and insects have been able to be restored thanks to the removal of alien predators such as rats and stoats. Zealandia has consequently developed into a significant refuge for species that are in danger of going extinct.

Visitors to Zealandia can stroll along a network of paths that wind through wetlands, native woods, and the Upper and Lower Dams, the sanctuary's main feature. You can view iconic New Zealand animals including the kiwi, takahe, and kaka while birdwatching in this peaceful location.

The visitor center showcases the sanctuary's commitment to education and community involvement with its interactive exhibits, informative displays, and treetop promenade. With the help of knowledgeable guides, Zealandia offers excursions that shed light on the ongoing efforts made by New

Zealand to preserve and restore its distinctive biodiversity.

In addition to its biological significance, Zealandia Ecosanctuary enhances Wellington's reputation as an environmentally conscious and green city. The sanctuary demonstrates the advantages of ecosystems devoid of predators and provides a model for long-term conservation techniques.

Going to Zealandia is an adventure into the core of New Zealand's conservation efforts, not just a walk in the woods. It's an opportunity to witness the resilience of native species, discover the interconnection of ecosystems, and take part in the ongoing discussion about environmental stewardship.

Wellington Waterfront

Wellington's waterfront is a vibrant, bustling area that captures the essence of the city's culinary, recreational, and cultural offerings. Stretching around the port, the waterfront has grown into a bustling area where locals and visitors alike go to socialize, unwind, and take in the best that Wellington has to offer.

One of the waterfront's unique features is its gorgeous promenade. Enjoy breath-inspiring views of the port, city skyline, and surrounding hills by taking a stroll along the waterfront. The visual tapestry is enhanced by sculptures, vibrant murals, and public artworks, resulting in an outdoor gallery that captures Wellington's creative spirit.

There are many different cafés, restaurants, and pubs along the waterfront, each offering a unique culinary experience. There are plenty of dining options to suit a variety of tastes, from contemporary coffee shops to seafood eateries on the shore. In Wellington, you should have lunch or a cup of coffee while admiring the harbor and far-off mountains.

Throughout the year, the waterfront is alive with festivals, events, and cultural celebrations. The TSB Arena and Shed 6 host conferences, exhibitions, and concerts, drawing a wide range of events that strengthen Wellington's standing as a cultural hub.

For those seeking recreational opportunities, the waterfront offers cycling, running, and even paddleboarding. Convenient bike rental stations allow visitors to explore the shoreline and its surroundings at their own pace.

The waterfront experience is given a literary touch by the renowned Wellington Writers Walk, which incorporates quotes from writers in New Zealand. It's a clever addition that goes well with Wellington's status as a UNESCO City of Literature.

The waterfront in Wellington is a living area that embodies the spirit of the city, not just a tourist destination. The waterfront invites everyone to partake in Wellington's liveliness and inventiveness, whether it's during a bustling cultural event, a romantic evening stroll, or a family picnic.

Mt. Victoria Lookout

The Mt. Victoria Lookout is an excellent vantage point for outstanding panoramic views of Wellington and its surroundings. Mt. Victoria, which rises 196 meters above sea level, affords a spectacular 360-degree view of the city, harbor, and surrounding surroundings.

Getting to the overlook is an experience in and of itself. Reaching the peak, whether by automobile, foot, or one of the various walking routes, promises to be a satisfying experience. The climb through thick vegetation, native plants, and glimpses of local animals adds to the excitement of the spectacular sights that lay at the summit.

When guests arrive at the overlook, they are treated to a panoramic view of Wellington's different landscapes. The central business area of the city, the flowing harbor, and the Cook Strait reaching towards the South Island present a spectacular perspective. The overlook is especially attractive around sunrise and dusk when the varying hues of the sky make a mesmerizing background.

The Mt. Victoria Lookout is more than just a tourist destination; it's an integral component of Wellington's outdoor culture. Locals and travelers often visit the summit for picnics, photography sessions, and peaceful introspection. The Wellington wind turbine, a unique symbol of the skyline, gives a sustainable energy component to the lookout's perspective.

Mt. Victoria features an extensive network of walking and mountain bike routes for those searching for a more active experience. The Southern Walkway, in particular, offers a lovely path connecting the overlook to other famous destinations such as the Wellington Botanic Garden and Oriental Bay.

The value of Mt. Victoria goes beyond its location as a magnificent viewpoint. It is a natural refuge inside the city that protects native plants and wildlife. The predator-free Zealandia fence, visible from the overlook, illustrates Wellington's dedication to ecological conservation.

In essence, the Mt. Victoria Lookout embodies Wellington's natural beauty as well as the city's spirit of adventure. It enables inhabitants and tourists to widen their horizons, experience the interaction of land and sea, and connect with the tough landscapes that characterize Wellington's character.

Wellington Zoo

Tucked away in Newtown's greenbelt, Wellington Zoo is a vibrant, animal-loving haven dedicated to conservation. The zoo was established in 1906 and has since developed into a modern, forward-thinking institution committed to animal care, education, and the advancement of human-animal interactions.

The Wellington Zoo offers far more than your average set of exhibits. It is a tour through the many habitats of animals from around the world as well as a celebration of New Zealand's unique wildlife. The zoo's advocacy for threatened species and participation in breeding programs meant to preserve genetic diversity are clear indications of its conservation efforts.

One of the zoo's highlights is the innovative Nest Te Khanga, which immerses visitors in New Zealand's unique ecosystems. Through educational exhibits, local bird habitats, and conservation initiatives, the region highlights the rich biodiversity of the nation.

There are giraffes, zebras, and meerkats in the zoo's Africa district for those who want up-close encounters with exotic animals. In the Wild Australia exhibit, guests can get up close and personal with native birds in a walk-through aviary as well as Australian wildlife like kangaroos and emus.

More than just a tourist destination, Wellington Zoo offers interaction and educational opportunities. By getting up close and personal with some of the zoo's animals through Close Encounters, visitors may better understand their unique characteristics and behaviors.

The zoo's environmental initiatives, which include garbage reduction, energy conservation, and habitat preservation, show how committed it is to sustainability. The Green Zoo initiative promotes environmentally friendly behaviors among visitors and inspires them to take up conservation activism.

Beyond its actual boundaries, Wellington Zoo is significant. To promote worldwide conservation efforts, it collaborates closely with both domestic and foreign organizations. The zoo's commitment to acting as a positive force for change is in line with Wellington's reputation as a green city.

Let's sum up by saying that Wellington Zoo offers more than just a variety of animal exhibits; it also acts as a venue for conservation efforts, education, and the growth of animal empathy. People can embark on a journey of education, appreciation, and advocacy for the welfare of all living creatures here.

The Beehive

The Executive Wing of the New Zealand Parliament Buildings, commonly referred to as The Beehive, is a piece of art and a representation of the nation's governing body. Sir Basil Spence's unique, beehive-shaped architecture is a monument to practicality and creativity. Completed in 1981, The Beehive houses the executive offices of the Prime Minister, members of the Cabinet, and other high-ranking government officials.

Through guided tours, guests can explore the Beehive's interior while learning about historical events, decision-making procedures, and the day-to-day activities of New Zealand's government. The unique circular Cabinet room, with its superb design and symbolic embellishments, enhances the attraction of this iconic structure.

Beyond its practical use, the Beehive enhances Wellington's architectural identity and serves as a physical representation of the nation's commitment to open governance. A thorough understanding of New Zealand's political structures can be gained from the nearby parliamentary complex, which houses the Parliamentary Debating Chamber and the Parliamentary Library.

a. Parliamentary Structures: Several structures within the Parliament Buildings complex serve as examples of how New Zealand's political landscape has developed. Constructed in the late 1800s, the historic Parliament House bears witness to the nation's history as a colony and its journey to self-government.

The Parliament Buildings offer fascinating guided tours through the historic halls, chambers, and passageways where important decisions shaping the history of the country have been made. Visitors gain insights into the complex tapestry of New Zealand's political past by touring places like the Grand Hall and the Legislative Council Chamber.

The main hub for legislative action is the recently constructed Parliament House, which is located close to the historic structures. Its clear and open style embodies the ideas of accessibility and responsibility. To get a deeper understanding of politics, visitors can watch debates and parliamentary sessions from the public galleries.

The well-maintained grass, statues, and monuments on the grounds offer a serene setting for reflection. The whole experience is enhanced by the Parliamentary Library, a treasure trove of knowledge and history.

b. Responses from Visitors: More than just a tour of the building's design and history, a visit to the Beehive and Parliament Buildings is an immersion into the democratic ideals that guide New Zealand's government. The knowledgeable guides provide context, anecdotes, and a deeper comprehension of the political systems of the country.

The Parliament Buildings and Beehive are physical embodiments of New Zealand democracy. The nation's ability to advance and adapt while preserving its political history is demonstrated by the blend of old and new architecture. As guests explore these sacred halls and watch the democratic process in action, they become significant characters in the ongoing narrative of New Zealand's government.

Ultimately, Wellington's Beehive and Parliament Buildings are more than just iconic structures; they are real-life examples of New Zealand's commitment to democracy, transparency, and public involvement. As essential components of the capital's urban landscape, these monuments provide tourists a chance to interact with the country's political history, inspiring a sense of collective accountability and pride in the democratic principles that characterize New Zealand.

CULTURAL ENCOUNTERS

Arts & Culture

Wellington's vibrant arts and cultural sector is a prime example of the city's inventiveness and commitment to fostering a vibrant cultural landscape. Both locals and visitors are drawn to the capital city of New Zealand because it offers a wide variety of cultural events, from galleries and exhibits to theaters and performing arts.

a. Theaters and Performing Arts:
Wellington boasts a rich and diverse theater scene that appeals to a broad spectrum of tastes and passions. From cutting-edge contemporary performances to historic plays

and international touring acts, the city's theaters and performance halls host a diverse array of events.

b. Te Whaea:

Also a center for performing arts education, Te Whaea is home to a range of theatrical productions. It is also known as the National Dance and Drama Centre. Among the state-of-the-art facilities are the renowned Toi Whakaari: New Zealand Drama School and the New Zealand School of Dance. A once-in-a-lifetime opportunity to witness the ingenuity and inventiveness emanating from New Zealand's performing arts scene is to attend a show at Te Whaea.

c. The Circa Theatre:

This well-known venue supporting New Zealand authors and performers is on the waterfront. Theater enthusiasts can find a modest theater at Circa Theatre, which focuses on producing top-notch, thought-provoking shows. The year-round varied schedule offers a blend of contemporary and classic performances.

d. St. James Theatre and the Opera House:

These two historic venues present a range of performing arts performances, such as dance, theater, and musical acts. These theaters' exquisite design and rich history lend an air of grandeur to Wellington's cultural landscape. Broadway-style plays, ballet, and opera are just a few of the world-class activities that take place in these venues.

Wellington is devoted to the performing arts in ways that go beyond traditional theaters. The arts are guaranteed to become a significant aspect of the city's identity through street performances, festivals, and outdoor events that contribute to the development of a lively and approachable cultural environment.

Galleries and Exhibitions

Wellington's exhibition spaces and art galleries create a colorful tapestry of regional and global artistic expressions. The city's galleries provide a forum for artistic and cultural exchange, featuring both contemporary installations and traditional art forms.

a. City Gallery Wellington:

City Gallery Wellington is a significant downtown modern art gallery. Numerous visual arts are on display, including multimedia installations, painting, sculpture, and photography. The gallery is at the forefront of Wellington's cultural landscape because of its commitment to pushing the boundaries of creativity and encouraging critical discourse.

b. Te Papa Art Gallery:

Te Papa Tongarewa, the country's museum, houses an art collection that encompasses both global and New Zealand creative influences. The gallery features European treasures, provocative contemporary pieces, and traditional and modern Maori art. The diverse programming makes sure that the abundance of New Zealand's creative output is always on show.

c. New Zealand Portrait Gallery:

For anyone interested in portraiture, the New Zealand Portrait Gallery is a fascinating experience. Situated on the waterfront, the gallery features portraits of well-known New Zealanders who tell stories about the history and cultural development of the nation.

Wellington's art districts, like Cuba Street and the Courtenay Place neighborhood, are dotted with smaller galleries, studios, and street art, all of which add to the city's eclectic and bohemian atmosphere. Wellington is committed to fostering and appreciating creativity, as seen by the yearly Wellington Art Walk and other cultural activities.

Maori Traditions

Wellington serves as a gateway to Maori culture, offering immersive experiences that shed light on the rich history and practices of New Zealand's indigenous people. The nation's capital provides a deep understanding of Maori culture through everything from historical Maori sites to cultural events.

a. Cultural displays:
Attending a traditional Maori cultural performance allows guests to interact with

the unique customs, storytelling, and performing arts of the Maori people. It's an interesting and educational experience.

b. Te Papa's Te Marae:
Te Papa Tongarewa's Te Marae is a dynamic representation of Maori culture. Cultural events including haka performances, song and dance storytelling, and traditional Maori welcoming ceremonies are held at the marae, or holy gathering place. These performances' immersive format offers an intimate and up-close look at Maori customs and hospitality.

c. Cultural Maori Performances:
Intriguing Maori traditional performances are available to tourists in Wellington in various venues. Among these are music,

dances from the past, and the powerful haka, a ceremonial dance that holds great cultural significance for the Maori people. Numerous performance groups, both within Te Papa and outside of independent cultural organizations, showcase the diversity and vibrancy of Maori performing arts.

Maori Heritage Sites

Maori heritage sites provide a more comprehensive understanding of the historical and cultural significance of Wellington and its environs to the Maori people.

a. Matiu and Somes Islands:
The Maori place Matiu/Somes Island in Wellington Harbor is of great cultural significance. Quarantine and military

defense are just two roles the island has played throughout history. While learning about the Maori history of the island and its local stories, visitors can take in the island's natural beauty.

b. Paekakariki Escarpment Track:

For those wishing to mix outdoor activities with Maori history, the Paekakariki Escarpment Track offers stunning views of the coastline and passes past Maori historical sites. Information about the customs, history, and tales of the nearby Maori settlements can be found on interpretative panels around the trail.

Wellington has demonstrated its commitment to acknowledging and preserving Maori culture by incorporating

Maori language, art, and stories throughout the city. From street names to public art installations, Wellington embraces and pays tribute to the cultural legacy of the tangata whenua (people of the land).

In summary, Wellington's cultural offerings, whether at galleries, theaters, or Maori traditional gatherings, create a rich and varied tapestry that embodies the city's dedication to the arts, inclusivity, and the honoring of its distinct cultural past.

OUTDOOR ACTIVITIES

Nature Walks and Hiking

Wellington is a haven for environment enthusiasts seeking hiking and trekking because of its rocky beach, verdant surroundings, and hills on all sides. You can re-establish a connection with nature at a short distance from the city center thanks to the diverse landscapes of the city, which offer a range of routes suitable for all skill levels.

a. Mount Kaukau:

For sweeping views of Wellington and the surroundings, the hike up Mount Kaukau is an absolute must. At 445 meters, it offers a challenging yet worthwhile climb. Reaching the summit rewards hikers with breathtaking views of the surrounding hills, port, and city. Mount Kaukau's varied geography, which includes open ridges and native vegetation, makes it a popular destination for locals seeking fun and fitness.

b. Mountain Bike Park at Makara Peak:

Although walking pathways wind through native woods and open spaces, Makara Peak is most renowned for its mountain biking routes. It's a great place for nature treks because of the many ecosystems; options range from easy strolls to strenuous climbs. The Tasman Sea and the South Island can be seen from the viewing spots on clear days.

c. Wellington Botanic Garden Trails:

The Wellington Botanic Garden serves as both a hiking haven and a botanical exhibit. A well-maintained walkway system flows through open meadows, natural forests, and themed gardens inside the garden. The Lady Norwood Rose Garden, Begonia House, and Treehouse Visitor Center are some of the sights along these peaceful strolling paths.

Wellington's outdoor trails are suitable for all types of walkers, from strolls to arduous treks, and provide an opportunity to escape the city and take in the surrounding natural beauty.

Cycling in Wellington

Wellington's compact size and dedicated bicycle infrastructure make it an ideal city to explore on two wheels. A wide range of city streets, beachside rides, and more challenging mountain bike paths are available to cyclists, providing an exciting and varied cycling experience.

a. Cycling along the Waterfront:

The Wellington waterfront is home to a picturesque bicycle track that stretches from Oriental Bay to the Hutt Valley. Cyclists may look out at the port, cycle past busy cafés, and enjoy the sea breeze. It offers a beautiful and accessible route and is suitable for cyclists of all ability levels due to the flat terrain.

b. Polhill Reserve Mountain Biking:

For those seeking a more daring riding experience, the Polhill Reserve offers a variety of difficult mountain bike routes. The trails wind through lush, natural flora, providing both satisfying climbs and exhilarating descents. The reserve is a well-liked option for cyclists looking to push their limits because of its proximity to the city core.

Water Sports

Wellington's coastal setting attracts those who enjoy the water to partake in a range of water activities, from kayaking to sailing. The port, bays, and other coastal regions offer a range of options for people seeking an aquatic adventure.

a. Sailing:

Wellington Harbor offers the perfect setting for enthusiasts of sailing. Both seasoned sailors and novices find the port to be a desirable location due to the dominant winds and its large waters. Sailing clubs and charters in the area offer sailing instruction and guided trips.

b. Kayaking:

Getting out on a kayak and exploring Wellington's coastline is a serene and intimate way to take in the natural beauty of the city. Between the protected waters of the port and the more adventurous coastal trails, kayakers can paddle past cliffs and coves and even witness marine life. There are guided kayaking outings and rental options available for all skill levels.

Day Trips to Surrounding Islands

Wellington is a great site to start day trips that offer an escape into nature and a variety of landscapes because of its proximity to stunning islands.

a. The Island of Kapiti:

Just a short boat ride and drive from Wellington, Kapiti Island is a refuge for native species free from predators. Joining a guided tour allows visitors to learn about conservation efforts, see rare bird species, and stroll the island's walking pathways. With its immaculate beaches and expansive views, Kapiti Island is a nature lover's dream come true.

b. Matiu and Somes Islands:

These islands, which are part of Wellington Harbor, are reserves with a rich past and a wide variety of wildlife. Reached by ferry, visitors can stroll along walking routes, see historic buildings, and take in stunning views of Wellington from the island. The island is a wonderful place for a day vacation because of its natural significance and tranquility.

Wellington's outdoor pursuits, whether on land or in the sea, offer the perfect ratio of adventure, leisure, and discovery. Because of the city's closeness to nature, both locals and visitors may venture outside and take in the variety of landscapes that truly set Wellington apart as a travel destination.

CUISINE AND DINING

The Culinary Scene in Wellington

The food scene in Wellington, the culinary capital of New Zealand, is vibrant and diverse, reflecting the city's creativity, originality, and commitment to quality ingredients. Nestled between hills and a gorgeous harbor, Wellington's food industry is as lively as its surroundings, offering a wide variety of dining options to suit all tastes and inclinations.

a. Culinary Innovation and Local Ingredients:
Wellington's food culture stands out for its combination of international cuisines and its emphasis on using fresh, local ingredients.

The city's chefs and culinary craftsmen enjoy sourcing fresh produce in season, seafood from nearby oceans, and premium meats from nearby farms. The commitment to utilizing products that are produced locally enhances the authenticity and freshness of Wellington's cuisine.

Wellington's culinary scene features chefs who are constantly experimenting with flavors, preparation techniques, and presentation. The city's dining options, which range from inventive street food vendors to upscale restaurants, offer a blend of locally produced food and cuisine with influences from across the world. Wellington has earned a reputation as a place where food is appreciated as an art form rather than a necessity because of this spirit of inquiry and inventiveness.

b. Culture of Coffee and Craft Beer:
Wellington is renowned for its artisan coffee and beer scenes. The city is home to several craft breweries that produce a wide range of drinks that showcase the creativity and passion of the regional brewing scene. In addition to sampling a variety of beers that pair well with Wellington's culinary offerings, visitors can explore craft beer trails.

Wellington has an equally excellent coffee culture. The city's coffee business is expanding as baristas showcase their skills in making the perfect pour-over, flat white, or espresso. Wellingtonians take their coffee very seriously, and the city's cafés are friendly hangouts where locals and visitors can enjoy a freshly brewed cup of coffee.

c. Waterfront Restaurants and Urban Eateries:

Wellington's waterfront is a well-liked dining spot with breathtaking views of the surrounding hills and harbor. For those seeking a gorgeous dining experience, waterfront restaurants provide a wide variety, ranging from casual fish & chip shops to elegant seafood restaurants.

Wellington's metropolitan sections, situated beyond the beach, are teeming with varied restaurants that contribute to the city's gastronomic tapestry. From modest bistros to trendy food zones, Wellington's culinary environment invites exploration and yields wonderful surprises at every turn.

To put it simply, Wellington's food industry captures the character of the city since it is creative, diverse, and deeply rooted in the environment. Wellington offers a culinary experience that celebrates the city's diverse tastes and culinary prowess, whether it is through fine dining, street food, or a craft brew by the shore.

Must Try Dishes

Wellington's food choices honor the distinctive cuisines of New Zealand and the city's commitment to culinary excellence. Many must-eats capture the essence of Wellington's culinary scene, from contemporary creations to traditional Kiwi fare.

a. Paua Fritters:

Wellington features the delectable pora (a type of abalone), which is a delicacy in New Zealand, in Paua Fritters. Herbs and spices are mixed with tenderized paua beef, which is then dipped in a thin batter and deep-fried till it turns golden brown. These fritters have a Kiwi spin on sea flavor, served with a squeeze of lemon.

b. Whitebait Fritters:

Another iconic New Zealand dish, Whitebait Fritters is made with tiny, translucent fish mixed with a thin batter made of eggs and fried to a soft crunch. Serve these fritters simply with a squeeze of lemon and a sprinkle of salt to bring out the natural sweetness of New Zealand seafood. A must-try for lovers of seafood.

c. Hangi:

If you want to sample real Maori cuisine, you have to eat hangi. A traditional method of cooking includes slow-cooking meat, vegetables, and occasionally fish in an earth oven. Consequently, the dish has a smoky and savory taste that aptly captures the essence of Maori cuisine. Several eateries in Wellington provide modern takes on Hangi so that patrons can experience this unique cooking technique.

d. Welling-Ton Ice Cream Burger

This is a well-known dessert that takes a peculiar twist on the traditional Kiwi burger.

It's a treat that consists of two delicious, Instagram-worthy donuts with homemade ice cream in between. It is a favorite among those who enjoy sweets because of its distinctive combination of flavors and textures.

e. Craft Burgers:

A multitude of upscale burger restaurants offering inventive concoctions are part of Wellington's burger culture, which is a culinary sensation. Wellington's artisan burgers, which come in a variety of flavors from lamb burgers with beetroot relish to vegetarian options made with fresh vegetables and local cheeses, are a testament to the city's love of quality ingredients and creative flavor combinations.

Popular Cafes and Restaurants

There is no shortage of restaurants and cafés in Wellington, and these establishments all help to make the city known as a gourmet haven. Wellington's eateries, which range from upscale dining establishments to cozy coffee shops, serve a wide range of interests and tastes.

a. Logan Brown:

A mainstay of Wellington's culinary scene for many years, Logan Brown is a well-known fine-dining establishment set in a gorgeously restored bank structure. Logan Brown is renowned for emphasizing locally grown and fresh ingredients in its sophisticated, yet classically inspired cuisine. Its elegant setting and first-rate service make it a fantastic choice for special occasions.

b. Ortega Fish House:

Located in the heart of Wellington, the Ortega Fish Shack is a seafood enthusiast's paradise. With a focus on using fresh, ethically sourced seafood, the restaurant's extensive menu features both inventive seafood dishes and traditional favorites like fish and chips. Ortega's welcoming atmosphere makes it a popular choice for both locals and visitors.

c. Loretta:

This hip cafe, located in the bustling Cuba Street district, blends a modern aesthetic with a commitment to serving seasonal, locally produced food. The menu features a broad selection of dishes, from sophisticated evening options to breakfast favorites. Because of its lovely decor and tranquil setting, Loretta is a well-liked restaurant for casual but elegant dining.

d. Flight Coffee Hangar:

The modern café and roastery that personifies Wellington's coffee culture is Flight Coffee Hangar. It takes its coffee very seriously. Exhibiting an industrial-chic vibe, Flight Coffee Hangar serves delicious brunch options along with beautifully brewed coffee. It's a local favorite for people who enjoy a nice cup of coffee in a laid-back setting.

e. Prefab:

A mainstay of Wellington's brunch scene, Prefab is an imaginative cafe and coffee roastery. Located in a repurposed warehouse, Prefab offers a wide range of cuisines to suit different dietary requirements. Prefab's emphasis on excellent coffee, freshly baked pastries, and extensive brunch selections have made it a go-to spot for people seeking a laid-back yet exciting dining experience.

Food Stores

The food markets in Wellington, which bring together regional producers, artisans, and food enthusiasts, are a lively display of the culinary diversity of the city. These markets transport you on a sensory journey filled with tastes, aromas, and the vibrant sense of community that defines Wellington's food scene.

a. Wellington Evening Market:
Wellington Night Market transforms Cuba Street into a gourmet carnival every Friday and Saturday night. Along with a multitude of cuisines, street food vendors, and live music, the market has it all. Delights from across the world, from Mediterranean delights to Asian street food, are available to visitors, fostering a vibrant and multicultural atmosphere.

b. The Harbourside Market:
Nestled against Wellington's waterfront, this Sunday morning mainstay is a fixture. The market features fresh veggies, handmade goods, local artisans, and an enticing array

of ready-to-eat treats. The best of the area's food is shown at the Harbourside Market, which offers everything from freshly prepared croissants to organic vegetables.

c. Chaffers Dock City Market:

Local chefs, producers, and culinary artists come together for the monthly Chaffers Dock City Market. Situated on a picturesque shoreline, the market offers a well-curated selection of fresh produce, delectable baked goods, and artisanal crafts. Meet the people who are driving Wellington's food scene and discover unique, locally made goods at this fantastic event.

d. Hill Street Farmers' Market:

For those looking for a market experience that emphasizes seasonal, fresh goods, the

Hill Street Farmers' Market is a must-see. This Thorndon-based market features a diverse range of merchants offering baked goods, artisanal cheeses, organic vegetables, and other goods. Its emphasis on sustainably sourced, locally produced products has made it a favorite among eco-aware foodies in Wellington.

Wellington's food markets are more than just places to shop; they are vibrant community hubs where locals and visitors can congregate to experience the breadth and depth of the city's culinary offerings. The markets invite guests to discover, sample, and engage with the essence of Wellington's culinary culture. They are a sensory extravaganza.

Ultimately, Wellington's dining and culinary scene is distinguished by a vibrant fusion of flavors, inventiveness, and close ties to regional resources. Wellington visitors can expect a gourmet journey that reflects the city's passion for food and dining culture, whether they are sampling well-known Kiwi specialties, exploring renowned cafés, or taking in the vibrant atmosphere of food markets.

ENTERTAINMENT AND NIGHTLIFE

Pubs and Bars

Wellington's nightlife offers a vibrant range of clubs and pubs that foster a vibrant and dynamic social scene. The city offers both contemporary cocktail bars and classic drinking spots, so there is something for everyone.

a. Mount Matterhorn:

Ever since the 1960s, Wellington's bar culture has been recognizable by the Matterhorn. This classy tavern in the heart of Cuba Street offers a unique blend of sophistication and casual appeal. The Matterhorn's creative beverages, carefully chosen wine list, and quirky design make it a top choice for anybody seeking a fun night out.

b. The Hawthorn Lounge:

If you're looking for a hint of old-world opulence, The Hawthorn Lounge is a hidden gem. Tucked down an alley off Tory Street, this speakeasy-style pub has a vintage vibe thanks to its opulent velvet seats and dim lighting. Professional mixologists craft classic and unique concoctions, creating an ideal setting for an elegant and exclusive night.

c. Vagabond and Rogue:

If you're looking for live music and specialty beer, go over to The Rogue and Vagabond. This busy pub in Te Aro Park regularly hosts live music events and has a large selection of specialty beers on tap. The informal outside dining area is a favorite among locals because it adds to the friendly atmosphere.

d. The Library Bar:

Located inside Wellington's historic Library, The Library Bar offers a setting with a literary feel. This bar provides a serene atmosphere for patrons to savor a range of beverages, including inventive cocktails and fine wines, with its book-lined walls and cozy nooks. Many choose the Library Bar when they're searching for a calm haven with a hint of sophistication.

Nightclubs

Wellington's nightclubs come alive as the sun sets, offering vibrant ambiance, heart-pounding music, and the chance to dance the night away. A diverse spectrum of tastes, from electronic dance music to eclectic sounds, are catered to in the city's nightclubs.

a. The Grand:

This upscale nightclub on Courtenay Place is well-known for its opulent interior design and exuberant vibe. The Grand, with its many dance floors, elite DJs, and elegant setting, welcomes partygoers looking for an immersive nightclub experience. The venue frequently hosts special events and themed evenings to heighten the excitement.

b. San Fran:

Also known as the San Francisco Bathhouse, San Fran is a lively nightclub that hosts live music performances. Its Cuba Street location draws a varied crowd with its extensive music selection, which features techno, indie, and alternative sounds. San Francisco's compact setting and lively dance floor make it a popular option for those seeking a more personal nightlife experience.

Live Music Venues

Wellington has a thriving and diverse live music scene, with venues presenting a wide range of genres from jazz and techno to indie rock and indie rock. These venues enhance the city's reputation as a hotspot for music.

a. Meow:

Meow is a hip live music venue with a cozy ambiance for music lovers, located on Edward Street. Meow's diverse programming, which features both local and international talent, has made it a favorite among those who enjoy a pleasant atmosphere and a variety of genres. The venue's attraction is enhanced by its commitment to supporting emerging artists.

b. Bodega:

Ghuznee Street's Bodega has long been a mainstay of Wellington's live music landscape. The venue hosts a range of events, such as techno musicians, rock stars, and indie bands. Because of its amazing sound system and lively atmosphere, Bodega has been known as the place to go if you want to see amazing live music.

Festivals and Cultural Events

Wellington's cultural calendar is jam-packed with festivals and events that showcase the city's vibrant arts scene and sense of community. These events, which range from film festivals to Mori culture celebrations, contribute to the capital's distinctive cultural fabric.

a. New Zealand Festival:

The New Zealand Festival is a biannual arts spectacular that transforms Wellington into a hub for the creative and cultural industries. A diverse array of performances in the areas of theater, dance, music, and visual arts are scheduled for the festival. One of Wellington's cultural highlights is the New Zealand Festival, which brings together national and international talent.

b. CubaDupa:

CubaDupa is a vibrant street festival that turns Cuba Street into a lively showcase of street performers, dancing, music, and art. The occasion draws both locals and visitors as it honors the distinctive and multicultural spirit of the city. CubaDupa is a prime example of Wellington's commitment to using cultural events to foster a sense of community, with its live music stages and vibrant parades.

c. Matariki:

Wellington celebrates Matariki, or the Maori New Year, with several events that pay tribute to Mori customs and culture. The festivities include storytelling, art exhibits, bonfires, and traditional performances. Matariki unites the community in remembrance of the past and celebration of their shared culture as they welcome the new year.

All things considered, Wellington's entertainment and nightlife options offer a wide variety of experiences, from sophisticated cocktails in stylish pubs to pulsating beats in energetic nightclubs. The city's love of live music and cultural events contributes to its reputation as a magnet for culture, where the arts and community come together to create evenings that both locals and visitors will never forget.

SHOPPING IN WELLINGTON

Boutique Shops

The myriad boutique establishments that line Wellington's charming streets set the city's retail scene apart. With everything from the stylish shops of Lambton Quay to the quirky businesses of Cuba Street, the city offers a distinctive and personalized shopping experience for anybody looking for something special and different.

a. Barkers:

A menswear brand from New Zealand that epitomizes contemporary style with a Kiwi touch, Barkers is situated on Lambton Quay. The store offers a wide range of clothing with a focus on quality and style, including casual wear and fitted suits. Because of its attention to detail and modern aesthetic, Barkers is a popular men's fashion store in Wellington.

b. Hunt & Seek:

This small business showcases independent and regional designers. It's on Cuba Street, which is a creative district. The carefully curated collection includes apparel, home goods, and accessories that are all committed to unique and sustainable design. The store is an excellent place to find emerging Kiwi talent because of its laid-back vibe and friendly staff.

c. The Service Depot:

For those who prefer classic and timeless styles, The Service Depot is a luxury menswear haven tucked away in the famed Old Bank Arcade. The store caters to people who appreciate quality craftsmanship and classic elegance by stocking carefully selected brands of everything from accessories to footwear.

d. Wanda Harland:

Located in the heart of the hipster haven that is the Cuba Street district, Wanda Harland is a store that combines gifts, home goods, and fashion. The store offers a distinctive and dynamic shopping experience because of its peculiar blend of globally sourced and locally created goods. The appeal is increased by Wanda Harland's commitment to supporting independent designers.

Wellington's shops contribute to the city's artistic and international atmosphere in addition to offering a unique shopping experience. These companies cater to discerning customers looking for distinctive and stylish products that prioritize quality, craftsmanship, and originality.

Craft Fairs and Markets

Wellington's markets and craft fairs offer an amazing array of locally made and produced goods, making for an intriguing shopping experience that transcends traditional retail settings. These markets showcase the ingenuity and sense of camaraderie that define Wellington's cultural landscape. They sell everything from fresh produce to artisan crafts.

a. Wellington Night Market:

Every Friday and Saturday night, Wellington Night Market turns Cuba Street into a bustling, colorful market that celebrates a variety of cuisines, handcrafted crafts, and live entertainment. Shops offering everything from clothing to jewelry to foreign street food are available for visitors to peruse. It is well-liked by locals and tourists alike because of its lively atmosphere and abundance of offerings.

b. Underground Market:

Situated in the underground parking structure of Jervois Quay, the Subterranean Market is a creative hub that features regional designers, artists, and craftspeople. A wide range of homemade goods, including jewelry, clothing, artwork, and accessories, are available at the market. Through direct interaction, visitors can learn about the creative processes behind each unique piece of art created by the makers.

c. The Hill Street Farmers' Market:

For those who enjoy artisanal treats and fresh cuisine, the Thorndon Hill Street Farmers' Market is a must-visit. Local farmers, growers, and food artisans get together for this weekly market to sell a wide range of seasonal fruits, vegetables, cheeses, baked goods, and other goods. The market is well-liked by Wellington's eco-conscious consumers because of its emphasis on sustainability and locally made goods.

d. Artisan Market at Craft Central:
Craft Central is a dedicated area within the Wellington Underground Market where artisans and craftspeople can showcase their handmade goods. Craft Central links regional producers with consumers seeking unique handcrafted goods, such as jewelry, medical supplies, textiles, and ceramics.

Local Products and Souvenirs

Thanks to Wellington's profusion of gift stores and boutiques that specialize in locally made goods, visitors may bring a little piece of the city's unique charm and cultural identity home with them. These companies offer a wide variety of mementos, from contemporary Kiwi designs to traditional Mori crafts.

a. The Te Papa Store:

Housed inside the iconic Te Papa Tongarewa (National Museum), the Te Papa Store is a veritable gold mine of souvenirs and handicrafts with Kiwi and Mori influences. Visitors can purchase traditional Mori carvings, pounamu (greenstone) jewelry, Kiwi-themed clothing, and a range of items that are a reflection of New Zealand's rich cultural history. The shop's merchandise offers a sincere approach to preserving memories of a trip to Wellington.

b. The Vault of Design:

Situated on Lombard Lane, The Vault Design Store is a haven for those in search of contemporary New Zealand design. The store offers a carefully curated selection of gifts, accessories, and home goods made in New Zealand that are all modern and stylish with a nod to Kiwi design. The Vault's emphasis on fine craftsmanship and imaginative design makes it a well-liked destination for unique gifts.

c. Coco Wellington:

This upscale chocolate shop provides imaginatively and painstakingly made artisan chocolates that add a sense of elegance and delight. The store's handcrafted creations, which range from truffles to chocolate bars, combine distinctive flavors and ingredients to make them a wonderful gift or treat for anybody with a sweet tooth.

d. Iko, Iko:

This distinctive and varied boutique, which is housed in the Cuba Street district, honors Kiwi tradition while incorporating contemporary elements. Unique gifts, stationery, and homeware with designs influenced by pop culture, New Zealand's flora, and wildlife are available at the shop. Iko Iko is a great location to purchase original souvenirs because of its amusing and inventive goods.

Wellington boasts a shopping culture that surpasses conventional retail establishments, featuring an eclectic assortment of boutiques, markets, and souvenir shops that showcase the creativity and craftsmanship of the locals. Whether perusing the artisanal wares at craft fairs or purchasing one-of-a-kind souvenirs from neighborhood shops, visitors to Wellington are sure to find objects that capture the essence of this vibrant city.

PRACTICAL
SUGGESTIONS

Payment and Currency

a. Currency:

The currency used in New Zealand is the New Zealand Dollar (NZD), also referred to as "$" or "NZ$." Coins are available in one and two-dollar denominations as well as 10, 20, and 50-cent denominations. There are notes available in 5, 10, 20, 50, and 100 dollar denominations.

b. Payment Methods:

Credit and debit cards are widely accepted in Wellington, especially in urban areas, large dining establishments, and retail establishments. Credit cards that are most frequently used are Visa and Mastercard; American Express and Diners Club cards are also accepted but are used less frequently. Always have some cash on hand, especially for smaller stores or markets where credit cards might not be accepted. ATMs are generally available to withdraw cash.

c. Currency conversion:
Services for exchanging currencies are offered by banks, currency exchange offices, and airports. ATMs make it simple to obtain local money, and banks frequently offer reasonable rates. To ensure you receive a good value for your money, keep an eye on currency rates.

Language

a. Official Language:

Wellington residents speak and understand English, which is the official language of New Zealand. Although English speakers may need some time to get used to the unique accent and some local slang, conversing should not be too tough.

b. Māori Language:

Although English is the primary language, the native Mori language has great cultural significance. There might be some Mori place names, greetings, and phrases. Even while you won't need to know many fundamental Mori words to have routine conversations, learning a few could improve your connections and cultural experiences.

Safety Recommendations

a. General Security:

Although basic precautions should always be taken, Wellington is known for being a safe city. Watch over your belongings, especially in crowded areas, and handle valuables with care. When exploring the city, be aware of your surroundings and take care of your hotel.

b. Weather Preparation:

Wellington's weather is erratic, with periods of strong winds and rain. It is advised to wear layers of clothing and pack a lightweight rain jacket. Comfortable walking shoes are recommended, especially if you plan to take a walking tour of the city.

c. Emergencies Services:

The emergency response system in New Zealand is dependable. In an emergency, dial 111 for police, fire, or ambulance assistance.

Local Etiquette

a. Cultural Awareness:

New Zealanders are renowned for their warmth and friendliness. Politeness and respect are highly valued in Kiwi culture. When speaking with locals, a simple "hello" or "kia ora" (the Mori greeting) goes a long way. Saying "please" and "thank you" is standard procedure in everyday interactions.

b. Indoor Shoes:

New Zealand homes and some traditional Mori settings typically require you to take off your shoes before entering. It's a good idea to follow your intuition if there's a pile of shoes by the door. Pay attention to cues.

c. Tipping:

Compared to other countries, New Zealanders tip less frequently. It is not necessary, but it is appreciated, especially for excellent service. Tipping is generally done by rounding up the bill or leaving a small amount.

d. Greetings:

In New Zealand, the most typical manner to welcome someone is with a handshake. When you are with friends or in more relaxed situations, a simple nod or wave will do. It's customary for close friends and family to give one other hug and cheek kisses.

To guarantee a positive and enjoyable trip to Wellington, it is important to comprehend and honor local customs and traditions. Kindness and openness are characteristic of Kiwis, and you will receive the same.

ITINERARIES

One-day itinerary

Explore Wellington for a day, flawlessly integrating cultural enrichment, natural beauty, and gastronomic pleasures.

Morning:

Begin at Fidel's Café:
Begin your day with a hearty breakfast at Fidel's Café, located on vibrant Cuba Street. Immerse yourself in a variety of cuisines, accompanied by a lively environment.

Expedition Te Papa Tongarewa:
Proceed to Te Papa Tongarewa, the National Museum that sits beautifully along the

coastline. Take a fascinating trip through New Zealand's rich past, as shown in stunning displays.

Afternoon:

Ascend by the Cable Car and enjoy a Garden Interlude:
Board the historic Wellington Cable Car for panoramic views from Kelburn's top. Explore the neighboring Wellington Botanic Garden, a lush urban hideaway, to find quiet.

Carter Observatory's Celestial Wonders:
Stroll through the Botanic Garden to the Carter Observatory. Immerse yourself in the mesmerizing universe of cosmic marvels with interactive displays and engaging planetarium programs.

Evening:

Street Vibrancy in Cuba:
Return to the vibrant Cuba Street for an unforgettable evening. Explore boutique shops, enjoy street entertainment, and take in the city's distinct cultural tapestry.

Logan Brown's Dinner Extravaganza:
Finish your day with a gastronomic marvel at Logan Brown, a prestigious restaurant located in a historic bank. Enjoy great food in an attractive environment.

Waterfront Relaxation with a Nightcap:
Finish your excursion with a walk around the shoreline, taking in the city lights. Enjoy a nightcap at one of the sophisticated waterside cafes.

Weekend Getaway in Wellington

Indulge in a weekend vacation that perfectly blends cultural learning, natural wonders, and gourmet delight.

Day 1:

Loretta's Brunch Elegance:
Begin your weekend with a delicious breakfast at Loretta, an upscale eatery on Cuba Street. Enjoy contemporary aesthetics and seasonal treats supplied locally.

Weta Workshop Reveals:
Visit Miramar for an exclusive Weta Workshop tour, which will give you a behind-the-scenes look at film production, special effects, and prop-making.

Afternoon:

Zealandia Wildlife Haven:
Spend the day in Zealandia, an ecosanctuary that showcases New Zealand's unique biodiversity. Guided tours provide information about conservation initiatives and the unique bird population.

Sunset View from Mount Victoria Lookout:
As the sun sets, climb to Mt. Victoria Lookout for panoramic views and a stunning sunset background, creating a lovely scene.

Evening:

Ortega Fish Shack's Seafood Festival:
Ortega Fish Shack's seafood feast will take you on a gourmet adventure. The

restaurant's dedication to fresh, sustainable seafood guarantees a pleasant dining experience.

Day 2:

Prefab's Morning Bliss:
Begin your second day with a delicious breakfast at Prefab, a modern coffee roastery that serves great coffee and a varied brunch menu.

Stroll around the Botanic Gardens and the Wellington Cable Car:
Spend the morning riding the Wellington Cable Car, then exploring the Wellington Botanic Garden at your leisure. Enjoy the tranquility of this urban sanctuary.

Afternoon:

Te Papa Tongarewa Cultural Immersion:
Spend the day exploring Te Papa Tongarewa's extensive collections. In this landmark museum, you may learn about New Zealand's natural history, Mori culture, and modern art.

Promenade along the water and a harbor cruise:
Take a relaxing walk around the Wellington Waterfront. Consider taking a harbor tour for a new viewpoint on marine treasures and gorgeous panoramas.

Evening:

Dragonfly's Culinary Finale:
Finish your weekend getaway with a refined meal at Dragonfly, a chic Asian fusion restaurant. Indulge in a variety of cuisine influenced by Southeast Asian tastes, a fitting gastronomic conclusion.

Extended Stay in Wellington

Extend your stay to completely immerse yourself in Wellington's diverse activities, which have been carefully handpicked to provide a seamless combination of cultural enrichment, outdoor adventure, and relaxing pleasures.

Week 1: Cultural Immersion

Waterfront Serenity and Te Papa Tongarewa:
Spend the first several days in Te Papa
Tongarewa, exploring its huge collections.
Enjoy leisurely seaside strolls while taking
in the unique cultural tapestry of the city.

Hidden Corners and Cuba Street Arts:
Explore the vibrant Cuba Street district,
looking for hidden jewels in stores, galleries,
and street performers. Immerse yourself in
the creative atmosphere of the city.

Mori Heritage and Geographic Exploration:
Explore Mori culture by visiting historical
sites and attending cultural events. Visit
surrounding places like Lower Hutt and

Petone to get a sense of the region's distinct personality.

Week 2: Nature Retreat and Recreational Activities

Botanic Bliss and Outdoor Adventures:
Spend unhurried days exploring the Wellington Botanic Garden's various landscapes. Investigate outdoor activities such as hiking, cycling, and water sports.

Relaxation and Island Excursion:
Take a day excursion to the surrounding islands and indulge in outdoor activities and moments of relaxation by the beach or in nature.

Shopping Spree and Unhurried Evenings:
Spend your last days shopping at boutiques, artisan markets, and leisurely nights. Explore the city's nightlife at your speed, uncovering hidden treasures, cultural events, and pubs.

This prolonged stay in Wellington allows you to immerse yourself in the city's cultural tapestry, natural attractions, and leisurely hobbies at your own pace.

CONCLUSION

In summary, Wellington is an exceptional place that skillfully blends culinary genius, scenic beauty, and cultural diversity. A continuous tapestry of sensations is created by every part of the city, from the vibrant streets of Cuba to the serene views of the Botanic Garden.

Admire the breathtaking views of the city's diverse terrain from the famous Cable Car, and immerse yourself in New Zealand's history at the National Museum, Te Papa Tongarewa. Wellington is a gourmet paradise, with everything from well-known local restaurants to elegant eating establishments.

No matter whether you're planning a weekend escape, a long weekend trip, or anything in between, Wellington has much to offer everyone's interests. A vibrant and satisfying visit is guaranteed by the city's commitment to preserving its history, valuing the natural world, and fostering a vibrant culture.

Enjoying the unique beauty and warmth of the capital is impossible to miss as the sun sets over Wellington Waterfront, casting a warm glow over the city's varied buildings. For those looking for a stunning mix of urban sophistication and natural beauty, Wellington beckons exploration and offers an engaging experience. For those fortunate enough to stroll its energetic streets, each moment becomes a chapter in a captivating story that unfolds inside the embrace of this dynamic city, creating a lasting memory.

Made in United States
North Haven, CT
20 December 2024

63111303R00085